COCKTAIL COLORING BOOK

THIS COLORING BOOK BELONGS TO:

_____

Jaylene Combs Design

COPYRIGHT © JAYLENE COMBS DESIGN 2021. SECOND EDITION 2024.

ALL RIGHTS RESERVED.

NO PART OF THIS PUBLICATION MAY BE REPRODUCED, DISTRIBUTED, OR TRANSMITTED IN ANY FORM OR BY ANY MEANS, INCLUDING PHOTOCOPYING, RECORDING, OR OTHER ELECTRONIC OR MECHANICAL METHODS, WITHOUT THE PRIOR WRITTEN PERMISSION OF THE PUBLISHER.

ILLUSTRATIONS, DESIGN, AND LAYOUT: JAYLENE COMBS

ISBN: 979-8593191601

MARGARITA

INGREDIENTS:
- 2 OZ TEQUILA
- 1 OZ TRIPLE SEC (ORANGE LIQUEUR)
- 1 OZ FRESH LIME JUICE
- ICE
- SALT FOR RIMMING THE GLASS (OPTIONAL)
- LIME WEDGE FOR GARNISH (OPTIONAL)

INSTRUCTIONS:
- IF DESIRED, RIM THE GLASS WITH SALT: RUB A LIME WEDGE AROUND THE RIM OF THE GLASS, THEN DIP IT ON A PLATE WITH SALT TO COAT THE RIM.
- FILL A SHAKER WITH ICE.
- POUR IN 2 OZ TEQUILA.
- ADD 1 OZ TRIPLE SEC (ORANGE LIQUEUR).
- SQUEEZE IN 1 OZ FRESH LIME JUICE.
- SHAKE VIGOROUSLY FOR ABOUT 10 SECONDS.
- STRAIN INTO THE PREPARED GLASS FILLED WITH ICE.
- GARNISH WITH A LIME WEDGE.

PALOMA

INGREDIENTS:
- 2 OZ TEQUILA (PREFERABLY BLANCO OR REPOSADO)
- 0.5 OZ FRESH LIME JUICE
- 3 OZ GRAPEFRUIT SODA
- ICE
- LIME WEDGE OR WHEEL FOR GARNISH (OPTIONAL)
- SALT FOR RIMMING THE GLASS (OPTIONAL)

INSTRUCTIONS:
- IF DESIRED, RIM A GLASS WITH SALT: RUB A LIME WEDGE AROUND THE RIM, THEN DIP IT ONT A PLATE WITH SALT TO COAT.
- FILL THE GLASS WITH ICE CUBES.
- POUR IN 2 OZ OF TEQUILA.
- SQUEEZE IN 0.5 OZ OF FRESH LIME JUICE.
- TOP OFF WITH 3 OZ OF GRAPEFRUIT SODA.
- STIR GENTLY TO MIX.
- GARNISH WITH A LIME WEDGE OR WHEEL.

MARTINI

INGREDIENTS:
- 2.5 OZ GIN OR VODKA
- 0.5 OZ DRY VERMOUTH
- ICE
- LEMON TWIST OR OLIVE FOR GARNISH (OPTIONAL)

INSTRUCTIONS:
- FILL A MIXING GLASS OR SHAKER WITH ICE.
- POUR IN 2.5 OZ OF GIN OR VODKA.
- ADD 0.5 OZ OF DRY VERMOUTH.
- STIR (OR SHAKE, IF PREFERRED) UNTIL WELL-CHILLED.
- STRAIN INTO A CHILLED GLASS.
- GARNISH WITH A LEMON TWIST OR AN OLIVE.

SIDECAR

INGREDIENTS:
- 2 OZ COGNAC OR BRANDY
- 0.75 OZ TRIPLE SEC (ORANGE LIQUEUR)
- 0.75 OZ FRESH LEMON JUICE
- ICE
- LEMON TWIST OR WEDGE FOR GARNISH (OPTIONAL)

INSTRUCTIONS:
- FILL A COCKTAIL SHAKER WITH ICE.
- POUR IN 2 OZ COGNAC OR BRANDY.
- ADD 0.75 OZ TRIPLE SEC (ORANGE LIQUEUR).
- SQUEEZE IN 0.75 OZ FRESH LEMON JUICE.
- SHAKE VIGOROUSLY FOR ABOUT 10 SECONDS.
- STRAIN INTO A CHILLED GLASS.
- GARNISH WITH A LEMON TWIST OR A LEMON WEDGE.

GIMLET

INGREDIENTS:
- 2 OZ GIN OR VODKA
- 0.75 OZ FRESH LIME JUICE
- 0.5 OZ SIMPLE SYRUP (EQUAL PARTS SUGAR AND WATER)
- ICE
- LIME WEDGE FOR GARNISH (OPTIONAL)

INSTRUCTIONS:
- FILL A COCKTAIL SHAKER WITH ICE.
- POUR IN 2 OZ GIN OR VODKA.
- SQUEEZE IN 0.75 OZ FRESH LIME JUICE.
- ADD 0.5 OZ SIMPLE SYRUP (SUGAR AND WATER MIXTURE).
- SHAKE VIGOROUSLY FOR ABOUT 10 SECONDS.
- STRAIN INTO A CHILLED GLASS.
- GARNISH WITH A LIME WEDGE.

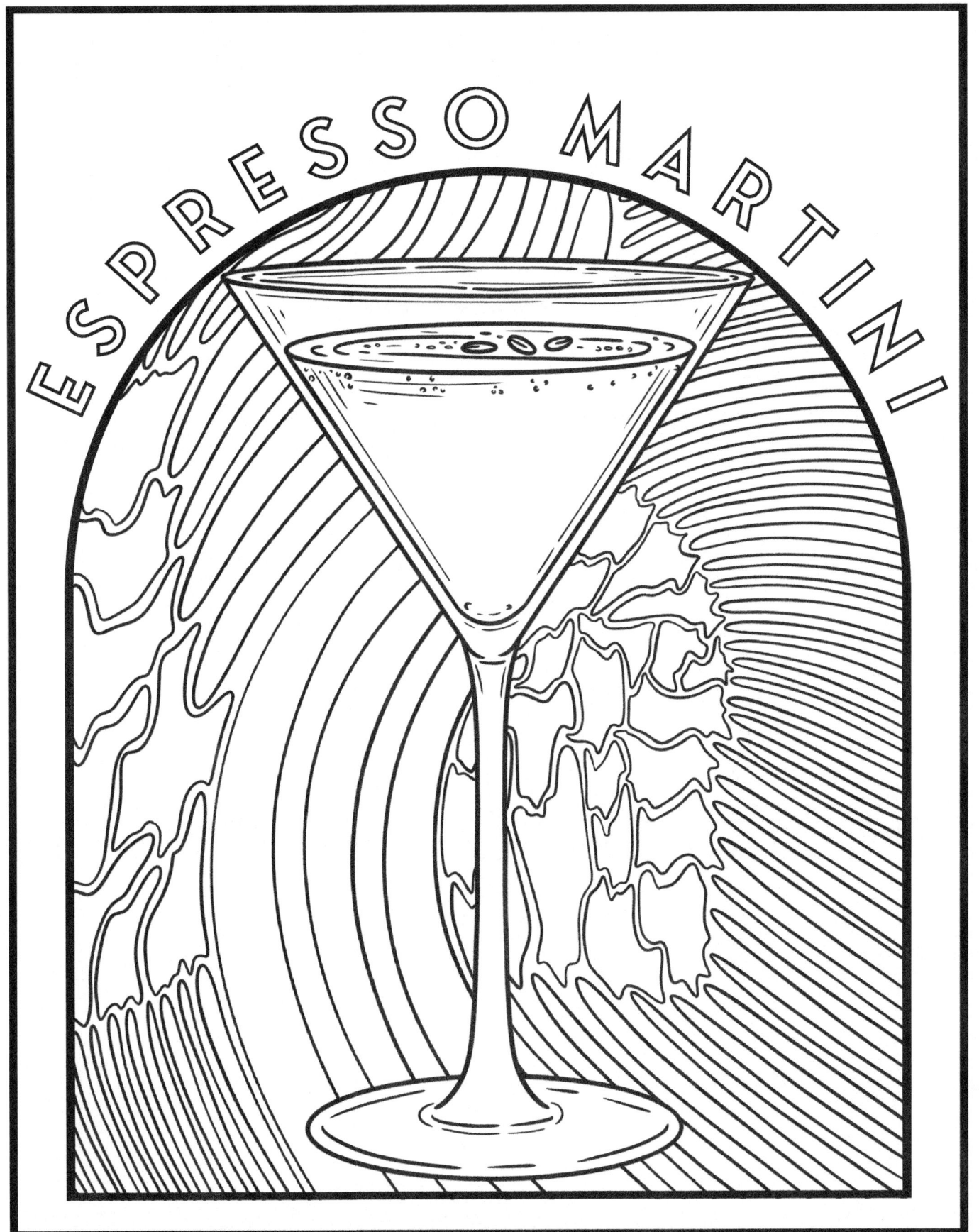

ESPRESSO MARTINI

INGREDIENTS:
- 1.5 OZ VODKA
- 1 OZ COFFEE LIQUEUR
- 1 OZ FRESHLY BREWED ESPRESSO (CHILLED)
- ICE
- 0.5 OZ SIMPLE SYRUP (EQUAL PARTS SUGAR AND WATER)
- COFFEE BEAN FOR GARNISH (OPTIONAL)

INSTRUCTIONS:
- FILL A COCKTAIL SHAKER WITH ICE.
- POUR IN 1.5 OZ VODKA.
- ADD 1 OZ COFFEE LIQUEUR
- ADD 1 OZ FRESHLY BREWED ESPRESSO (CHILLED).
- ADD 0.5 OZ SIMPLE SYRUP.
- SHAKE VIGOROUSLY FOR ABOUT 10 SECONDS.
- STRAIN INTO A CHILLED GLASS.
- GARNISH WITH A COFFEE BEAN.

BLOODY MARY

INGREDIENTS:
- 1.5 OZ VODKA
- 3 OZ TOMATO JUICE
- 0.5 OZ LEMON JUICE
- DASH OF HOT SAUCE (ADJUST TO TASTE)
- ICE
- DASH OF WORCESTERSHIRE SAUCE (ADJUST TO TASTE)
- PINCH OF SALT AND PEPPER
- CELERY STALK AND LEMON WEDGE FOR GARNISH (OPTIONAL)

INSTRUCTIONS:
- FILL A GLASS WITH ICE.
- POUR IN 1.5 OZ VODKA.
- ADD 3 OZ TOMATO JUICE.
- SQUEEZE 0.5 OZ LEMON JUICE.
- ADD A DASH OF HOT SAUCE (ADJUST TO YOUR SPICE PREFERENCE).
- ADD A DASH OF WORCESTERSHIRE SAUCE.
- SEASON WITH A PINCH OF SALT AND PEPPER.
- STIR WELL.
- GARNISH WITH A CELERY STALK AND A LEMON WEDGE.

TOM COLLINS

INGREDIENTS:
- 2 OZ GIN
- 1 OZ FRESH LEMON JUICE
- 0.5 OZ SIMPLE SYRUP (EQUAL PARTS SUGAR AND WATER)
- CLUB SODA
- ICE
- LEMON WHEEL AND MARASCHINO CHERRY FOR GARNISH (OPTIONAL)

INSTRUCTIONS:
- FILL A GLASS WITH ICE.
- POUR IN 2 OZ GIN.
- SQUEEZE IN 1 OZ FRESH LEMON JUICE.
- ADD 0.5 OZ SIMPLE SYRUP (SUGAR AND WATER MIXTURE).
- TOP OFF WITH CLUB SODA TO YOUR DESIRED LEVEL.
- STIR GENTLY TO MIX THE INGREDIENTS.
- GARNISH WITH A LEMON WHEEL AND A MARASCHINO CHERRY.

COSMOPOLITAN

INGREDIENTS:
- 1.5 OZ VODKA
- 0.5 OZ TRIPLE SEC (ORANGE LIQUEUR)
- 0.5 OZ CRANBERRY JUICE
- 0.25 OZ FRESH LIME JUICE
- ICE
- LIME TWIST OR ORANGE PEEL FOR GARNISH (OPTIONAL)

INSTRUCTIONS:
- FILL A COCKTAIL SHAKER WITH ICE.
- POUR IN 1.5 OZ VODKA.
- ADD 0.5 OZ TRIPLE SEC (ORANGE LIQUEUR).
- ADD 0.5 OZ CRANBERRY JUICE.
- SQUEEZE IN 0.25 OZ FRESH LIME JUICE.
- SHAKE VIGOROUSLY FOR ABOUT 10 SECONDS.
- STRAIN INTO A GLASS.
- GARNISH WITH A LIME TWIST OR AN ORANGE PEEL.

TEQUILA SUNRISE

INGREDIENTS:
- 2 OZ TEQUILA
- 4 OZ ORANGE JUICE
- 0.5 OZ GRENADINE SYRUP
- ICE
- ORANGE SLICE AND MARASCHINO CHERRY FOR GARNISH (OPTIONAL)

INSTRUCTIONS:
- FILL A GLASS WITH ICE.
- POUR IN 2 OZ TEQUILA.
- ADD 4 OZ ORANGE JUICE.
- SLOWLY DRIZZLE 0.5 OZ GRENADINE SYRUP OVER THE BACK OF A SPOON OR BY TILTING THE GLASS TO CREATE A SUNRISE EFFECT.
- LET THE GRENADINE SETTLE AT THE BOTTOM OF THE GLASS.
- GARNISH WITH AN ORANGE SLICE AND A MARASCHINO CHERRY.

DAIQUIRI

INGREDIENTS:
- 2 OZ WHITE RUM
- 1 OZ FRESH LIME JUICE
- 0.5 OZ SIMPLE SYRUP (EQUAL PARTS SUGAR AND WATER)
- ICE

INSTRUCTIONS:
- FILL A COCKTAIL SHAKER WITH ICE.
- POUR IN 2 OZ WHITE RUM.
- SQUEEZE IN 1 OZ FRESH LIME JUICE.
- ADD 0.5 OZ SIMPLE SYRUP (SUGAR AND WATER MIXTURE).
- SHAKE VIGOROUSLY FOR ABOUT 10 SECONDS.
- STRAIN INTO A CHILLED GLASS.

MOJITO

INGREDIENTS:
- 2 OZ WHITE RUM
- 1 OZ FRESH LIME JUICE
- 2 TEASPOONS SUGAR (OR TO TASTE)
- 6-8 FRESH MINT LEAVES
- CLUB SODA
- ICE
- LIME WEDGE AND MINT SPRIG FOR GARNISH (OPTIONAL)

INSTRUCTIONS:
- IN A GLASS, MUDDLE THE FRESH MINT LEAVES AND SUGAR TOGETHER TO RELEASE THE MINT'S AROMA.
- SQUEEZE IN 1 OZ OF FRESH LIME JUICE.
- ADD 2 OZ OF WHITE RUM.
- FILL THE GLASS WITH ICE CUBES.
- TOP OFF WITH CLUB SODA.
- STIR GENTLY TO MIX THE INGREDIENTS AND DISSOLVE THE SUGAR.
- GARNISH WITH A LIME WEDGE AND A SPRIG OF MINT.

NEGRONI

INGREDIENTS:
- 1 OZ GIN
- 1 OZ CAMPARI
- 1 OZ SWEET VERMOUTH
- ICE
- ORANGE TWIST OR SLICE FOR GARNISH (OPTIONAL)

INSTRUCTIONS:
- FILL A MIXING GLASS WITH ICE.
- POUR IN 1 OZ GIN.
- ADD 1 OZ CAMPARI.
- ADD 1 OZ SWEET VERMOUTH.
- STIR GENTLY TO COMBINE.
- STRAIN INTO A GLASS FILLED WITH ICE.
- GARNISH WITH AN ORANGE TWIST OR A SLICE.

OLD FASHIONED

INGREDIENTS:
- 2 OZ BOURBON OR RYE WHISKEY
- 1 SUGAR CUBE
- 2 DASHES ANGOSTURA BITTERS
- ICE
- ORANGE TWIST AND CHERRY FOR GARNISH (OPTIONAL)

INSTRUCTIONS:
- PLACE A SUGAR CUBE IN A GLASS.
- ADD 2 DASHES OF ANGOSTURA BITTERS ONTO THE SUGAR CUBE.
- MUDDLE THE SUGAR AND BITTERS TOGETHER TO DISSOLVE.
- FILL THE GLASS WITH ICE.
- POUR IN 2 OZ OF BOURBON OR RYE WHISKEY.
- STIR GENTLY TO COMBINE.
- GARNISH WITH AN ORANGE TWIST AND A CHERRY.

BEE'S KNEES

INGREDIENTS:
- 2 OZ GIN
- 0.75 OZ HONEY SYRUP (EQUAL PARTS HONEY AND HOT WATER)
- 0.75 OZ FRESH LEMON JUICE
- ICE
- LEMON TWIST OR TWIST OF LEMON PEEL FOR GARNISH (OPTIONAL)

INSTRUCTIONS:
- FILL A COCKTAIL SHAKER WITH ICE.
- POUR IN 2 OZ OF GIN.
- ADD 0.75 OZ OF HONEY SYRUP (HONEY AND HOT WATER MIXTURE).
- SQUEEZE IN 0.75 OZ OF FRESH LEMON JUICE.
- SHAKE VIGOROUSLY FOR ABOUT 10 SECONDS.
- STRAIN INTO A CHILLED GLASS.
- GARNISH WITH A LEMON TWIST OR A TWIST OF LEMON PEEL.

SEX ON THE BEACH

INGREDIENTS:
- 1.5 OZ VODKA
- 0.5 OZ PEACH SCHNAPPS
- 2 OZ CRANBERRY JUICE
- 2 OZ ORANGE JUICE
- ICE
- ORANGE SLICE AND MARASCHINO CHERRY FOR GARNISH (OPTIONAL)

INSTRUCTIONS:
- FILL A GLASS WITH ICE.
- POUR IN 1.5 OZ VODKA.
- ADD 0.5 OZ PEACH SCHNAPPS.
- POUR 2 OZ CRANBERRY JUICE.
- ADD 2 OZ ORANGE JUICE.
- STIR GENTLY TO MIX THE INGREDIENTS.
- GARNISH WITH AN ORANGE SLICE AND A MARASCHINO CHERRY.

WHISKEY SOUR

INGREDIENTS:
- 2 OZ WHISKEY (BOURBON OR RYE)
- 0.75 OZ FRESH LEMON JUICE
- 0.5 OZ SIMPLE SYRUP (EQUAL PARTS SUGAR AND WATER)
- ICE
- LEMON WHEEL OR CHERRY FOR GARNISH (OPTIONAL)

INSTRUCTIONS:
- FILL A COCKTAIL SHAKER WITH ICE.
- POUR IN 2 OZ WHISKEY.
- ADD 0.75 OZ FRESH LEMON JUICE.
- ADD 0.5 OZ SIMPLE SYRUP (SUGAR AND WATER MIXTURE).
- SHAKE VIGOROUSLY FOR ABOUT 10 SECONDS.
- STRAIN INTO A GLASS FILLED WITH ICE.
- GARNISH WITH A LEMON WHEEL OR A CHERRY.

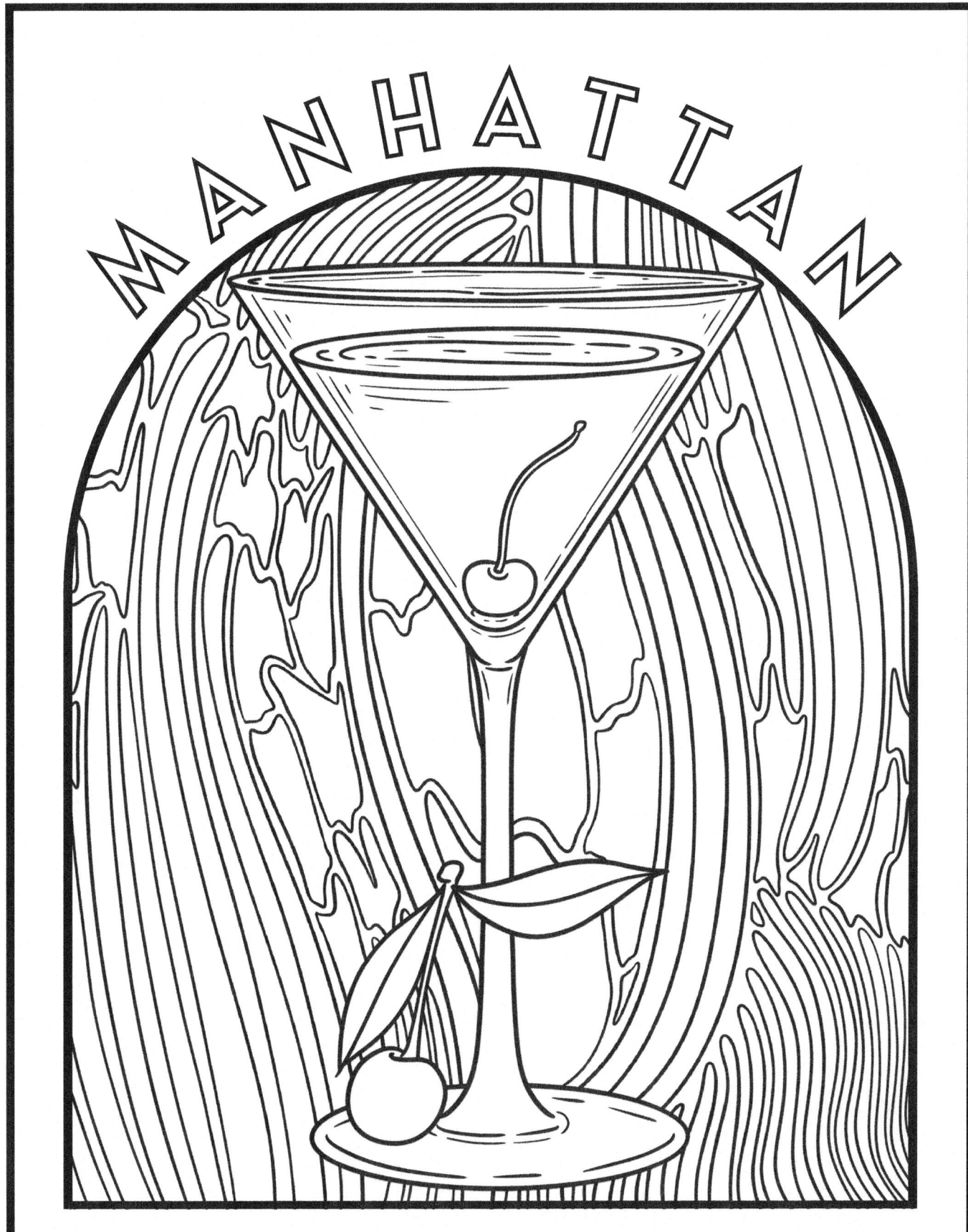

MANHATTAN

INGREDIENTS:
- 2 OZ BOURBON OR RYE WHISKEY
- 1 OZ SWEET VERMOUTH
- 2-3 DASHES ANGOSTURA BITTERS
- ICE
- MARASCHINO CHERRY FOR GARNISH (OPTIONAL)

INSTRUCTIONS:
- FILL A MIXING GLASS WITH ICE.
- ADD 2 OZ WHISKEY.
- POUR IN 1 OZ SWEET VERMOUTH.
- ADD 2-3 DASHES OF ANGOSTURA BITTERS.
- STIR WELL.
- STRAIN INTO A CHILLED GLASS.
- GARNISH WITH A MARASCHINO CHERRY.

GIN & TONIC

INGREDIENTS:
- 2 OZ GIN
- 4-6 OZ TONIC WATER
- ICE
- LIME OR LEMON WEDGE

INSTRUCTIONS:
- FILL A GLASS WITH ICE.
- POUR 2 OZ GIN.
- ADD 4-6 OZ TONIC WATER.
- SQUEEZE A LIME OR LEMON WEDGE.

SANGRIA

INGREDIENTS:
- 1 BOTTLE (750 ML) RED WINE
- 1/4 CUP BRANDY OR ORANGE LIQUEUR
- 1/4 CUP ORANGE JUICE
- 1/4 CUP SIMPLE SYRUP (EQUAL PARTS SUGAR AND WATER)
- 1 ORANGE, THINLY SLICED
- 1 LEMON, THINLY SLICED
- 1 LIME, THINLY SLICED
- 1 APPLE, CORED AND DICED
- ICE
- 1 CUP CLUB SODA OR LEMON-LIME SODA (CHILLED)

INSTRUCTIONS:
- IN A LARGE PITCHER, COMBINE THE RED WINE, BRANDY OR ORANGE LIQUEUR, ORANGE JUICE, AND SIMPLE SYRUP.
- ADD THE THINLY SLICED ORANGE, LEMON, AND LIME TO THE MIXTURE.
- GENTLY STIR TO COMBINE ALL THE INGREDIENTS.
- REFRIGERATE FOR AT LEAST 2 HOURS, ALLOWING THE FLAVORS TO MELD.
- JUST BEFORE SERVING, ADD THE DICED APPLE AND THE CHILLED CLUB SODA OR LEMON-LIME SODA.
- STIR GENTLY.
- SERVE IN GLASSES FILLED WITH ICE AND GARNISH WITH ADDITIONAL FRUIT SLICES IF DESIRED.

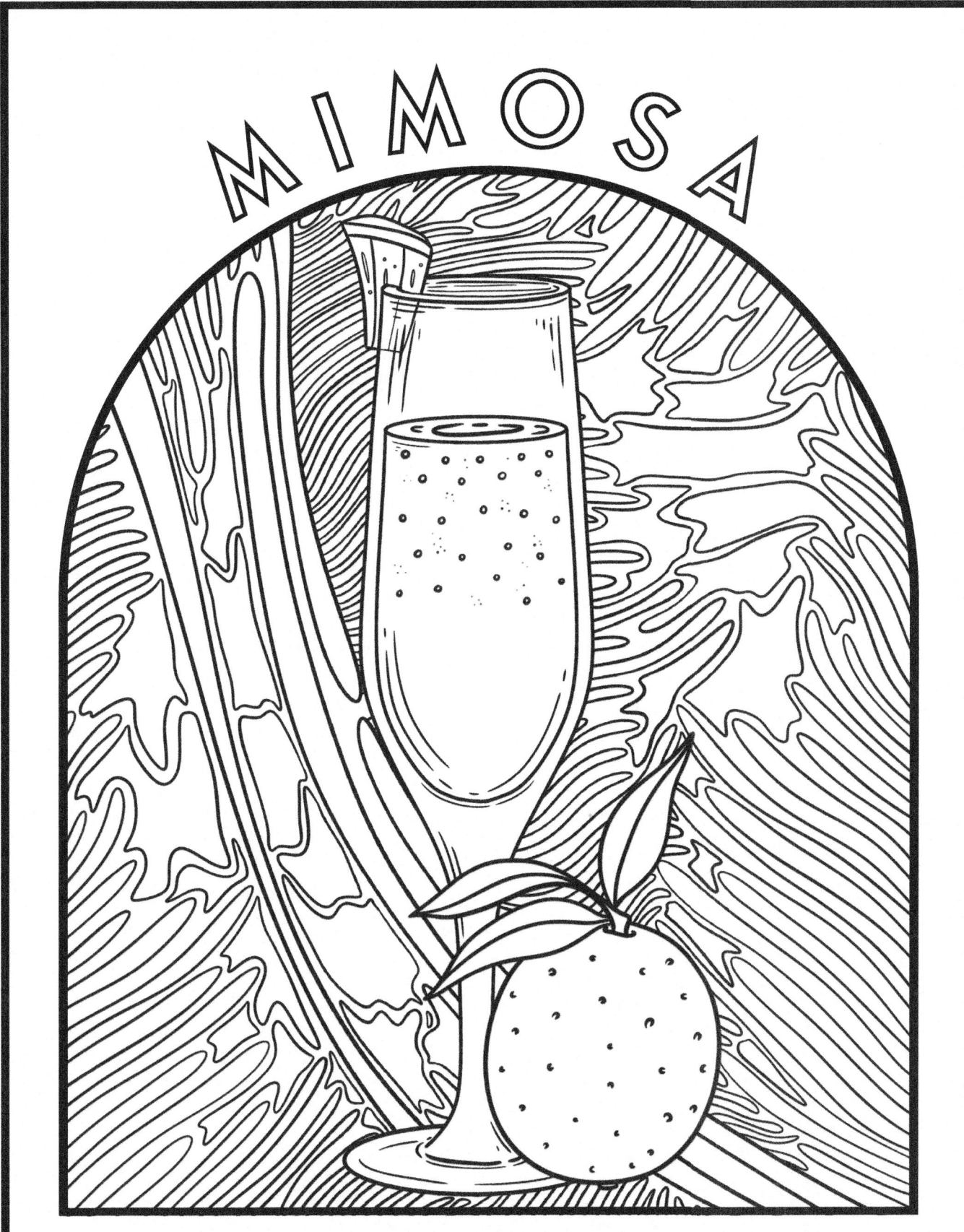

MIMOSA

INGREDIENTS:
- 2 OZ CHILLED CHAMPAGNE OR SPARKLING WINE
- 2 OZ CHILLED ORANGE JUICE
- ORANGE SLICE OR TWIST FOR GARNISH (OPTIONAL)

INSTRUCTIONS:
- FILL A GLASS WITH 2 OZ OF CHILLED CHAMPAGNE OR SPARKLING WINE.
- SLOWLY POUR IN 2 OZ OF CHILLED ORANGE JUICE.
- GENTLY STIR TO COMBINE.
- GARNISH WITH AN ORANGE SLICE OR TWIST.

BLUE LAGOON

INGREDIENTS:
- 1.5 OZ VODKA
- 0.5 OZ BLUE CURAÇAO LIQUEUR
- LEMONADE OR CLUB SODA
- ICE
- LEMON WHEEL OR CHERRY FOR GARNISH (OPTIONAL)

INSTRUCTIONS:
- FILL A GLASS WITH ICE.
- POUR IN 1.5 OZ VODKA.
- ADD 0.5 OZ BLUE CURAÇAO LIQUEUR.
- TOP OFF WITH LEMONADE OR CLUB SODA TO YOUR DESIRED LEVEL.
- STIR GENTLY TO MIX THE INGREDIENTS AND CREATE A VIBRANT BLUE COLOR.
- GARNISH WITH A LEMON WHEEL OR A CHERRY.

SCREWDRIVER

INGREDIENTS:
- 2 OZ VODKA
- 4 OZ ORANGE JUICE
- ICE
- ORANGE SLICE FOR GARNISH (OPTIONAL)

INSTRUCTIONS:
- FILL A GLASS WITH ICE.
- POUR IN 2 OZ VODKA.
- ADD 4 OZ ORANGE JUICE.
- STIR GENTLY TO COMBINE.
- GARNISH WITH AN ORANGE SLICE.

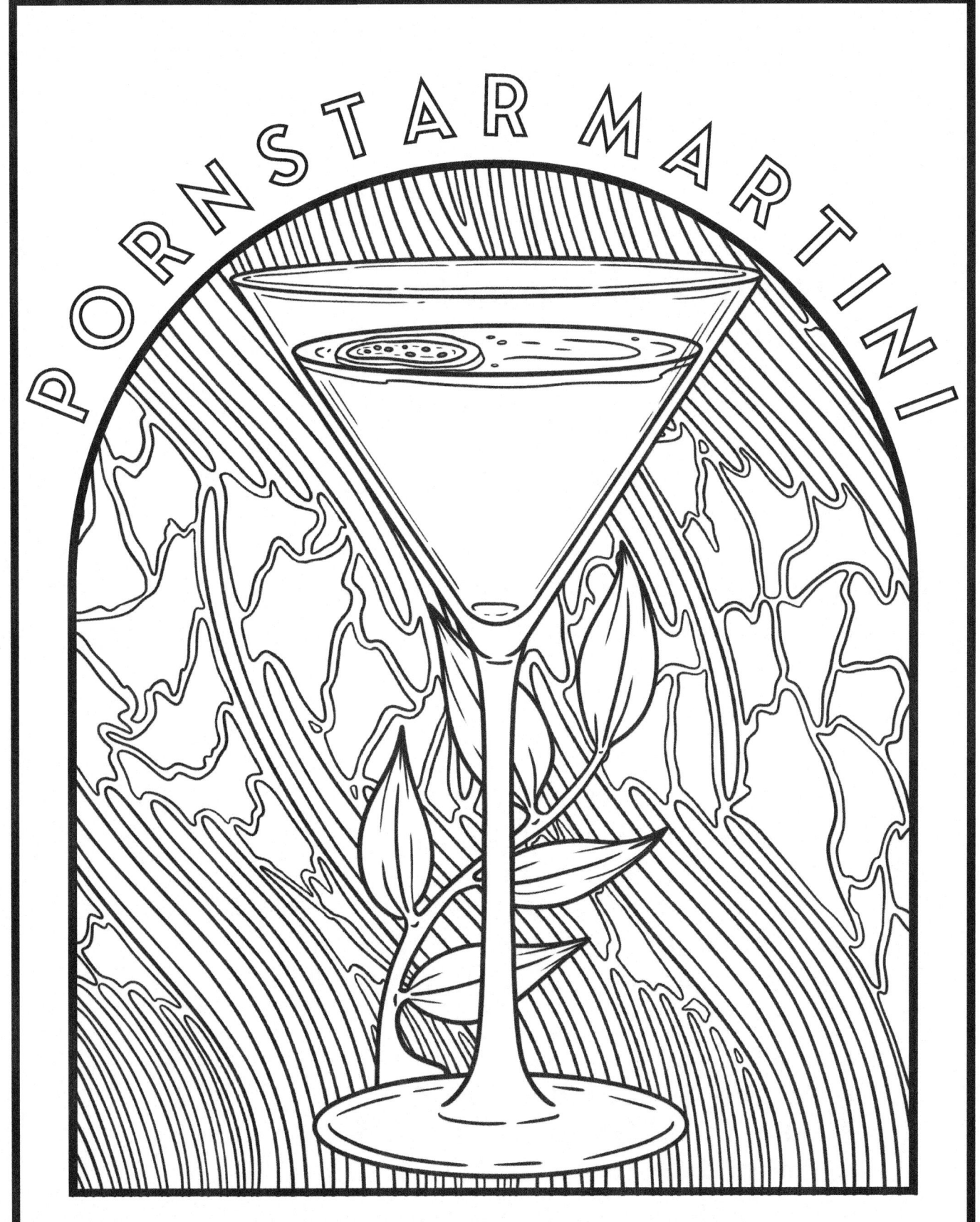

PORNSTAR MARTINI

INGREDIENTS:
- 1.5 OZ VANILLA VODKA
- 0.5 OZ PASSION FRUIT LIQUEUR
- 1 OZ PASSION FRUIT PUREE
- 0.5 OZ SIMPLE SYRUP (EQUAL PARTS SUGAR AND WATER)
- 0.5 OZ FRESH LIME JUICE
- ICE
- SLICE OF PASSION FRUIT FOR GARNISH (OPTIONAL)
- A SHOT OF CHILLED PROSECCO OR CHAMPAGNE (SERVED ON THE SIDE)

INSTRUCTIONS:
- FILL A COCKTAIL SHAKER WITH ICE.
- POUR IN 1.5 OZ VANILLA VODKA.
- ADD 0.5 OZ PASSION FRUIT LIQUEUR.
- ADD 1 OZ PASSION FRUIT PUREE.
- ADD 0.5 OZ SIMPLE SYRUP (SUGAR AND WATER MIXTURE).
- ADD 0.5 OZ FRESH LIME JUICE.
- SHAKE VIGOROUSLY FOR ABOUT 10 SECONDS.
- STRAIN INTO A GLASS.
- CUT THE SLICE OF PASSION FRUIT INTO QUARTERS AND FLOAT ONE QUARTER IN THE DRINK.
- SERVE WITH A SHOT OF CHILLED PROSECCO OR CHAMPAGNE ON THE SIDE.

MOSCOW MULE

INGREDIENTS:
- 2 OZ VODKA
- 4 OZ GINGER BEER
- 0.5 OZ FRESH LIME JUICE
- ICE
- LIME WEDGE OR WHEEL FOR GARNISH (OPTIONAL)

INSTRUCTIONS:
- FILL A COPPER MOSCOW MULE MUG OR GLASS WITH ICE CUBES.
- POUR IN 2 OZ VODKA.
- ADD 0.5 OZ FRESH LIME JUICE.
- TOP OFF WITH 4 OZ GINGER BEER.
- STIR GENTLY TO COMBINE.
- GARNISH WITH A LIME WEDGE OR WHEEL.

APEROL SPRITZ

INGREDIENTS:
- 3 OZ APEROL
- 2 OZ PROSECCO
- 1 OZ CLUB SODA
- ICE
- ORANGE SLICE OR TWIST FOR GARNISH (OPTIONAL)

INSTRUCTIONS:
- FILL A GLASS WITH ICE.
- POUR IN 3 OZ OF APEROL.
- ADD 2 OZ OF PROSECCO.
- TOP OFF WITH 1 OZ OF CLUB SODA.
- STIR GENTLY TO COMBINE.
- GARNISH WITH AN ORANGE SLICE OR TWIST.

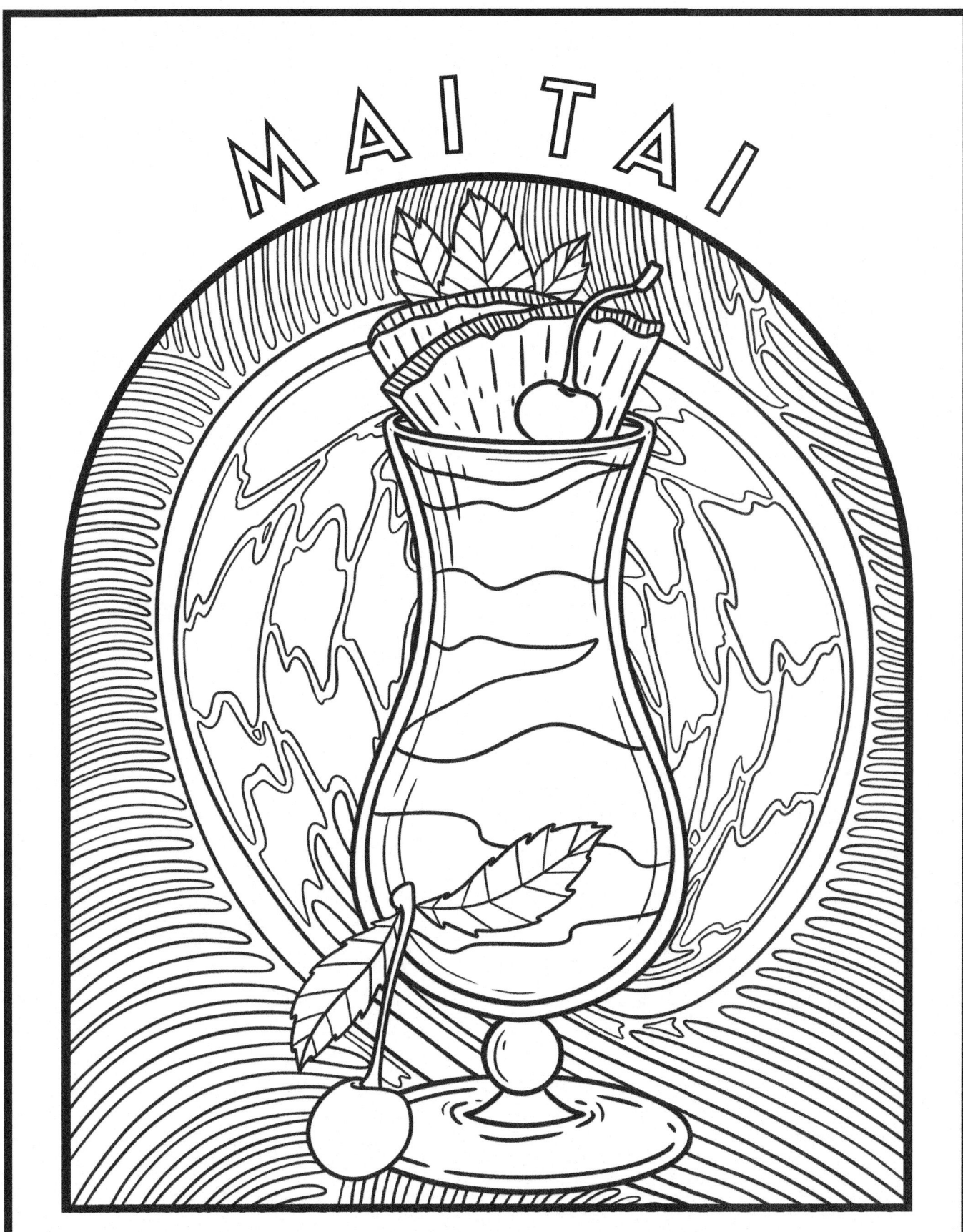

MAI TAI

INGREDIENTS:
- 2 OZ LIGHT RUM
- 0.75 OZ LIME JUICE
- 0.5 OZ ORANGE LIQUEUR
- 0.25 OZ ORGEAT SYRUP
- ICE
- 0.25 OZ SIMPLE SYRUP (EQUAL PARTS SUGAR AND WATER)
- LIME WHEEL, PINEAPPLE, CHERRY, AND MINT SPRIG FOR GARNISH (OPTIONAL)

INSTRUCTIONS:
- FILL A COCKTAIL SHAKER WITH ICE.
- POUR IN 2 OZ LIGHT RUM.
- ADD 0.75 OZ LIME JUICE.
- ADD 0.5 OZ ORANGE LIQUEUR.
- ADD 0.25 OZ ORGEAT SYRUP.
- ADD 0.25 OZ SIMPLE SYRUP (SUGAR AND WATER MIXTURE).
- SHAKE VIGOROUSLY FOR ABOUT 10 SECONDS.
- STRAIN INTO A GLASS FILLED WITH ICE.
- GARNISH WITH A LIME WHEEL, PINEAPPLE, CHERRY, AND A SPRIG OF MINT.

LONG ISLAND ICED TEA

INGREDIENTS:
- 0.5 OZ VODKA
- 0.5 OZ RUM
- 0.5 OZ GIN
- 0.5 OZ TEQUILA
- 0.5 OZ TRIPLE SEC (ORANGE LIQUEUR)
- 1 OZ FRESH LEMON JUICE
- 1 OZ SIMPLE SYRUP (EQUAL PARTS SUGAR AND WATER)
- COLA TO TOP OFF
- ICE
- LEMON WHEEL FOR GARNISH (OPTIONAL)

INSTRUCTIONS:
- FILL A GLASS WITH ICE.
- POUR IN 0.5 OZ VODKA.
- ADD 0.5 OZ RUM.
- ADD 0.5 OZ GIN.
- ADD 0.5 OZ TEQUILA.
- ADD 0.5 OZ TRIPLE SEC (ORANGE LIQUEUR).
- SQUEEZE IN 1 OZ FRESH LEMON JUICE.
- ADD 1 OZ SIMPLE SYRUP (SUGAR AND WATER MIXTURE).
- STIR GENTLY TO MIX THE INGREDIENTS.
- TOP OFF WITH COLA TO FILL THE GLASS.
- GARNISH WITH A LEMON WHEEL.

PEACH BELLINI

INGREDIENTS:
- 2 OZ PEACH PUREE OR PEACH NECTAR
- 4 OZ CHILLED PROSECCO OR CHAMPAGNE
- PEACH SLICE OR RASPBERRY FOR GARNISH (OPTIONAL)

INSTRUCTIONS:
- POUR 2 OZ OF PEACH PUREE OR PEACH NECTAR INTO CHILLED GLASS.
- SLOWLY TOP OFF WITH 4 OZ OF CHILLED PROSECCO OR CHAMPAGNE.
- STIR GENTLY TO COMBINE, IF DESIRED.
- GARNISH WITH A PEACH SLICE OR A RASPBERRY.

PIÑA COLADA

INGREDIENTS:
- 2 OZ WHITE RUM
- 3 OZ PINEAPPLE JUICE
- 1 OZ COCONUT CREAM
- ICE
- PINEAPPLE SLICE AND MARASCHINO CHERRY FOR GARNISH (OPTIONAL)

INSTRUCTIONS:
- FILL A BLENDER WITH ICE.
- POUR IN 2 OZ WHITE RUM.
- ADD 3 OZ PINEAPPLE JUICE.
- ADD 1 OZ COCONUT CREAM.
- BLEND UNTIL SMOOTH.
- POUR INTO A CHILLED GLASS.
- GARNISH WITH A PINEAPPLE SLICE AND A MARASCHINO CHERRY.

Thank You!

THANK YOU FOR SUPPORTING AN INDEPENDENT PUBLISHER! WE INVITE YOU TO SHARE YOUR THOUGHTS BY LEAVING A REVIEW AND ENCOURAGE YOU TO CHECK OUT OUR OTHER BOOKS. YOUR CONTINUED SUPPORT ALLOWS US TO BRING YOU MORE UNIQUE ART.

About The Illustrator

JAYLENE COMBS IS AN ILLUSTRATOR AND DESIGNER FROM THE UNITED STATES. SHE FINDS INSPIRATION IN THE SIMPLE JOYS OF LIFE. WHEN SHE'S NOT MAKING ART, JAYLENE ENJOYS READING BOOKS, PETTING CATS, AND COOKING. SHOP MORE OF HER ART IN OTHER JAYLENE COMBS DESIGN COLORING BOOKS AND AT WWW.MIDNIGHTDOORSTUDIO.COM.

Printed in Great Britain
by Amazon